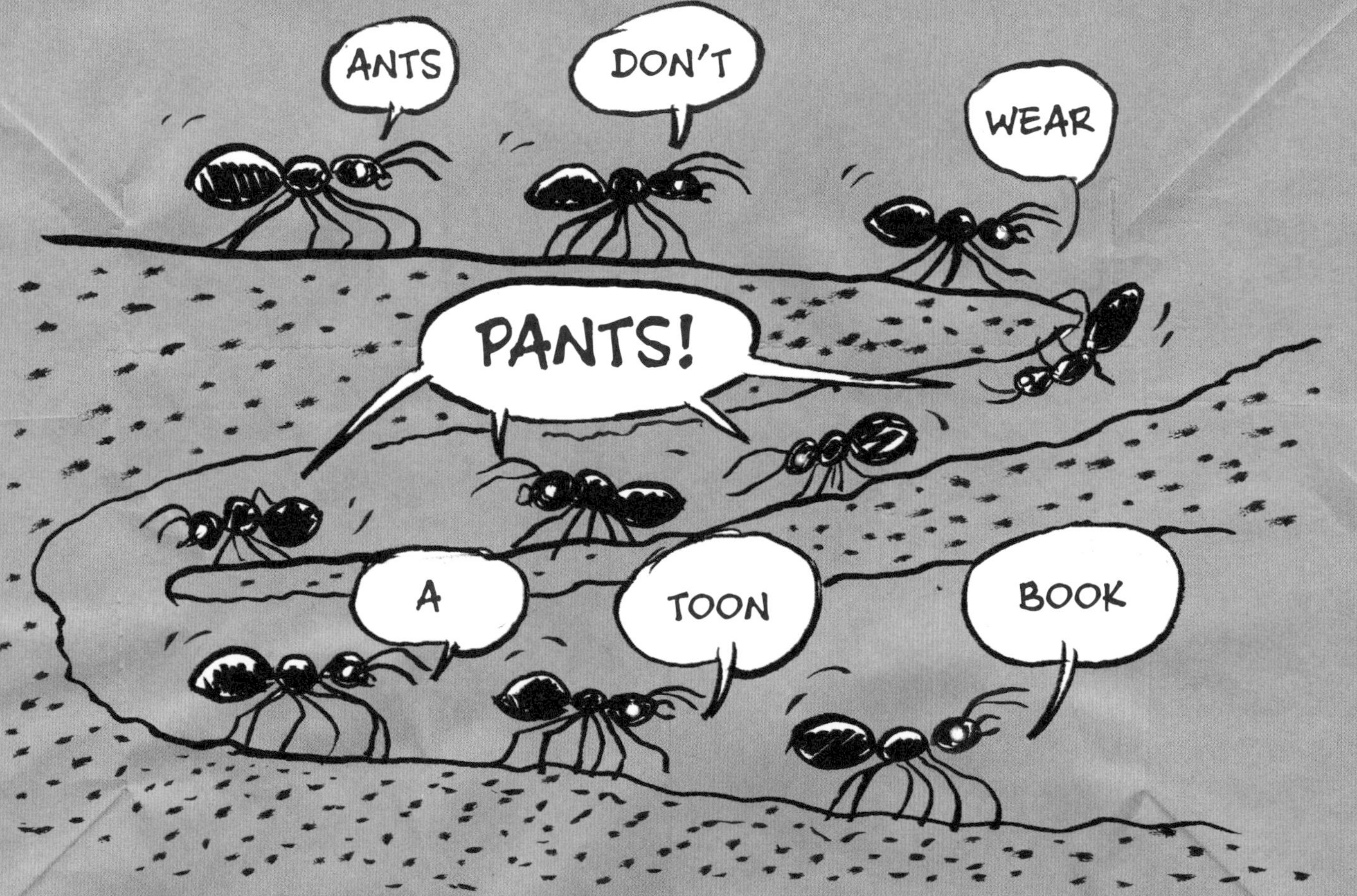
ANTS
DON'T
WEAR
PANTS!
A
TOON
BOOK

KEVIN McCLOSKEY

TOON BOOKS • NEW YORK

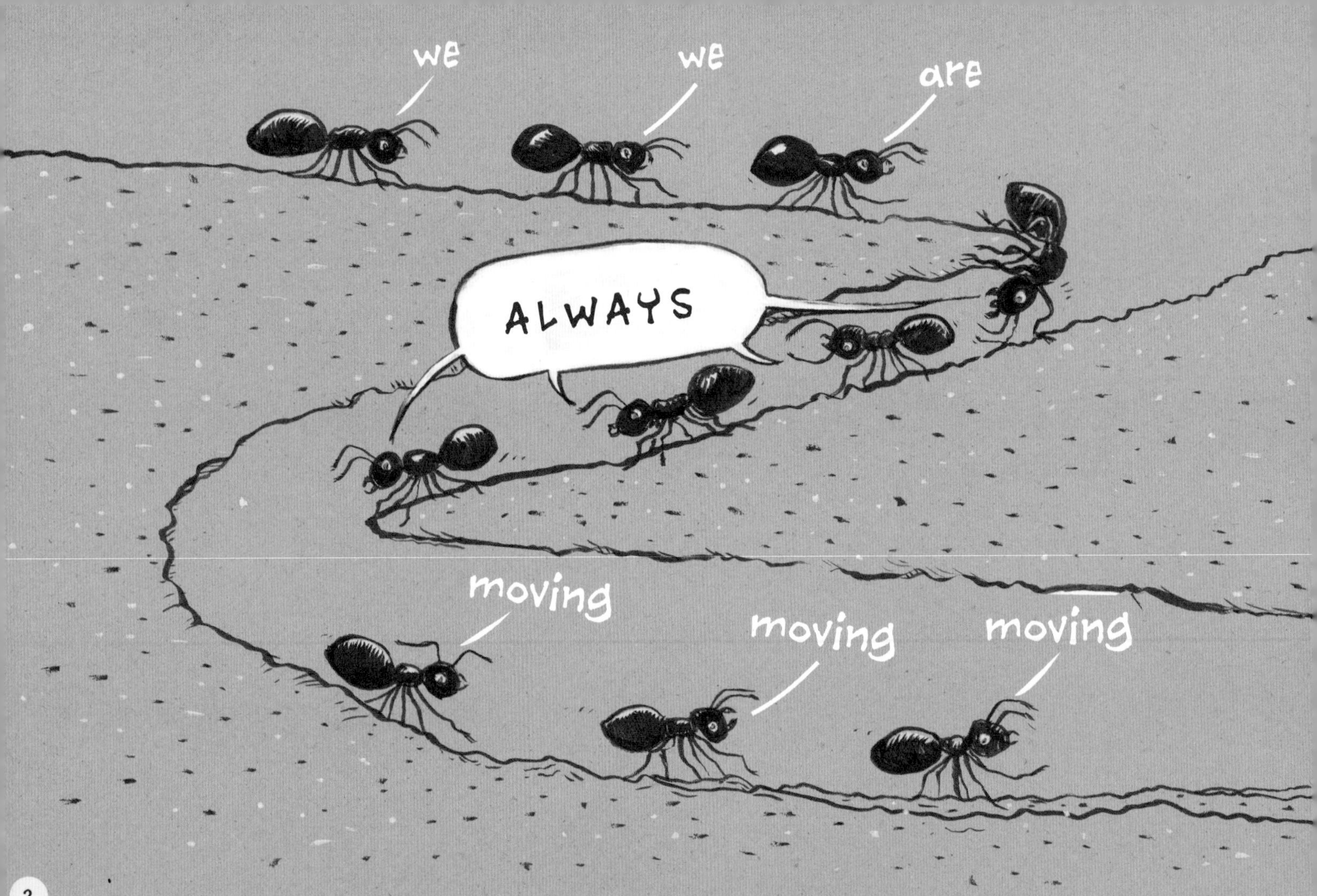
we
we
are
ALWAYS
moving
moving
moving

WHEN YOU CAN'T STOP MOVING,
WE SAY YOU HAVE "ANTS IN YOUR PANTS."

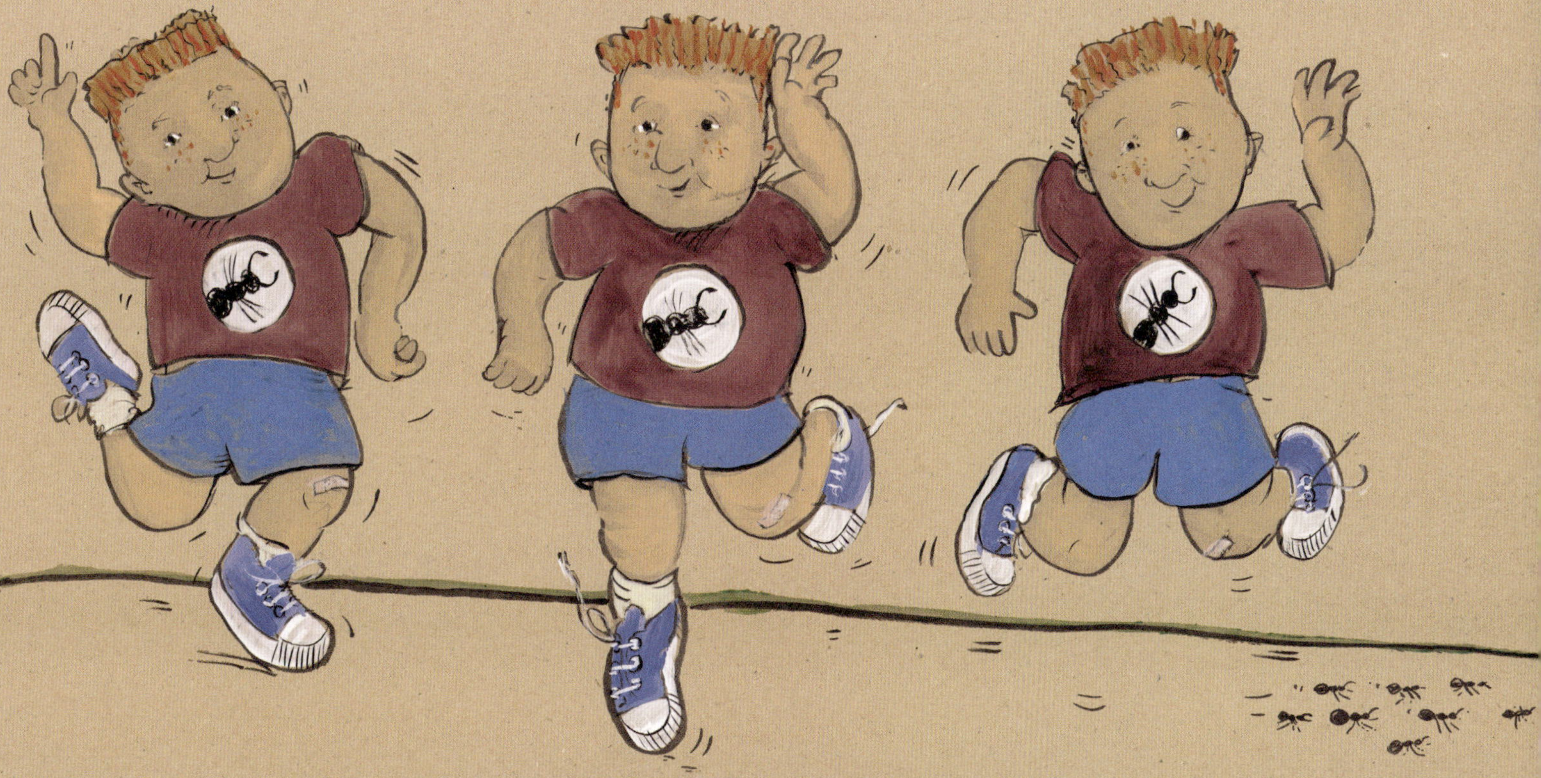

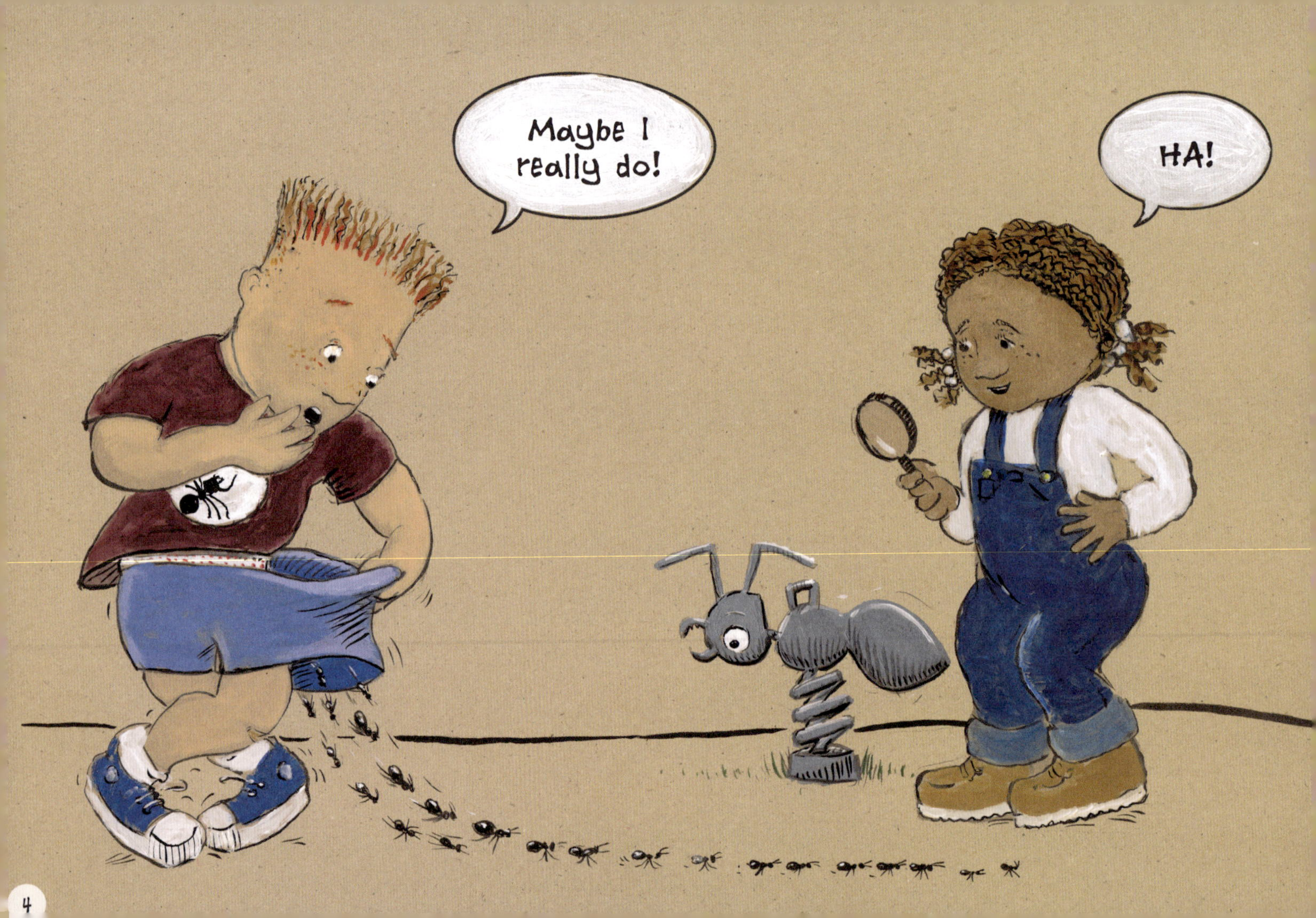
Maybe I really do!
HA!

ANTS ARE ALL AROUND US. LOOK AND YOU WILL FIND ANTHILLS.

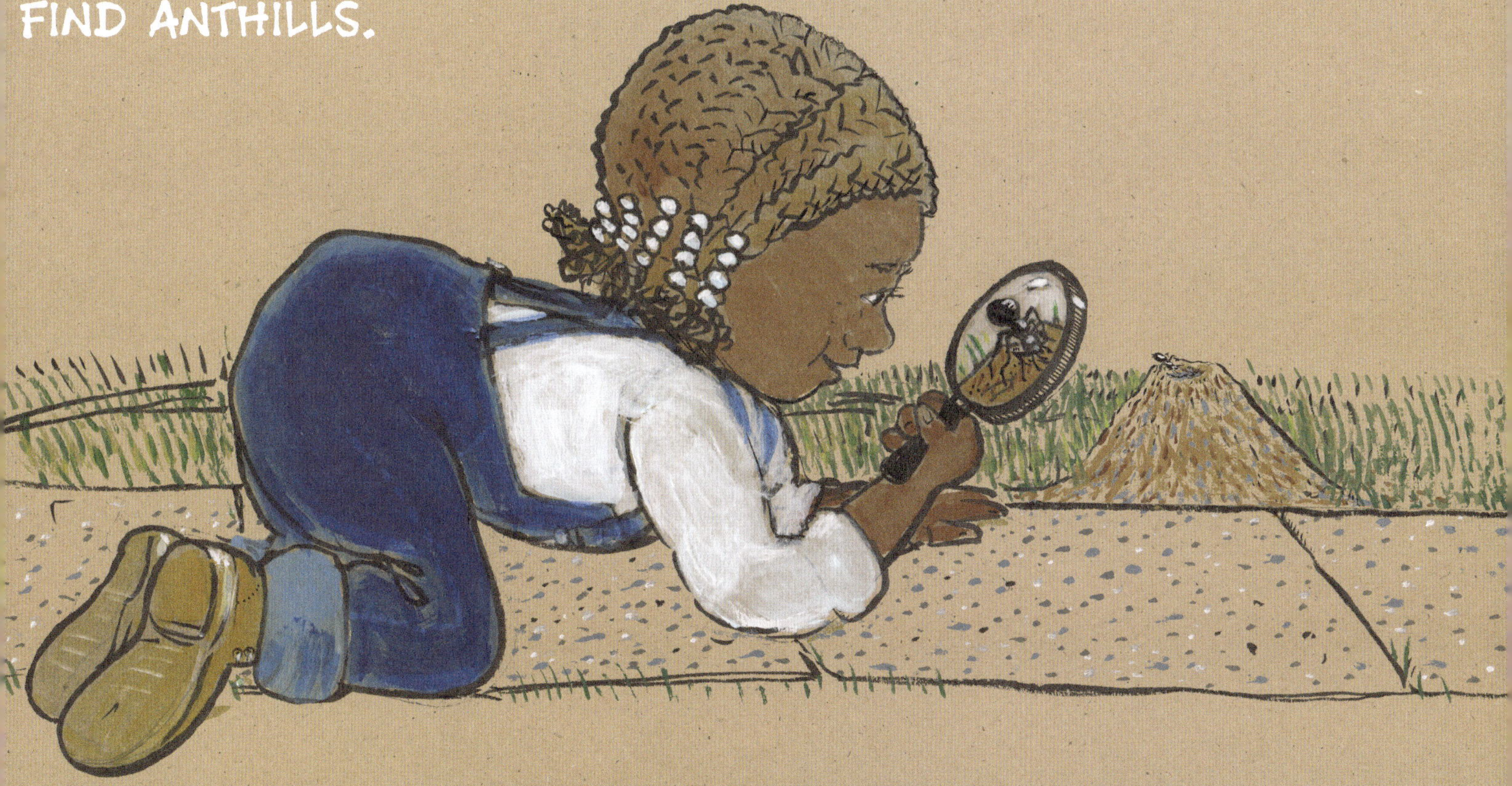

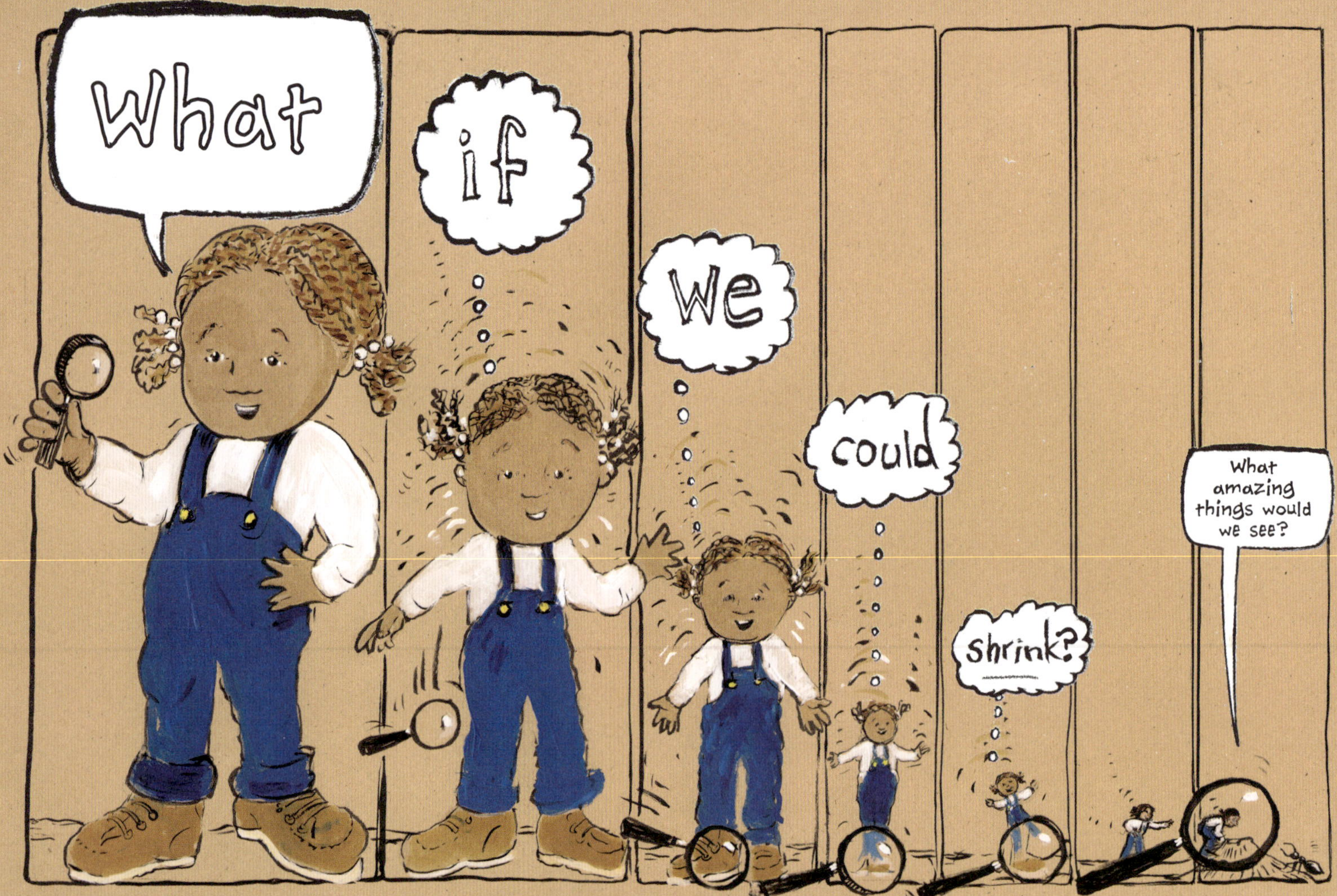
What
if
we
could
shrink?
What amazing things would we see?

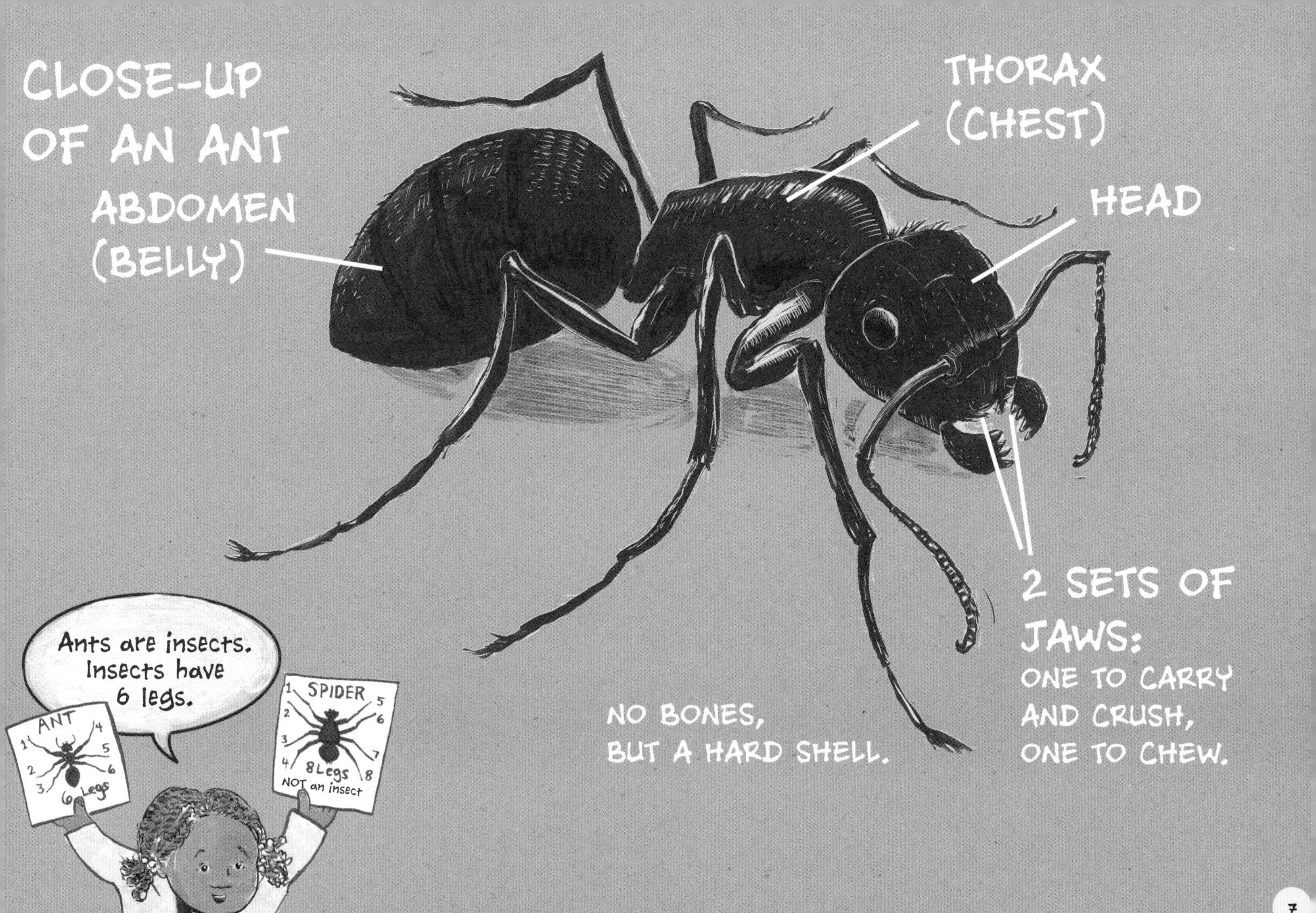
CLOSE-UP OF AN ANT
ABDOMEN (BELLY)
THORAX (CHEST)
HEAD
2 SETS OF JAWS: ONE TO CARRY AND CRUSH, ONE TO CHEW.
NO BONES, BUT A HARD SHELL.
Ants are insects. Insects have 6 legs.
ANT
1
2
3
4
5
6
6 Legs
SPIDER
1
2
3
4
5
6
7
8
8 Legs
NOT an insect

ANTS HAVE TWO STOMACHS.
ONE IS JUST FOR SHARING.

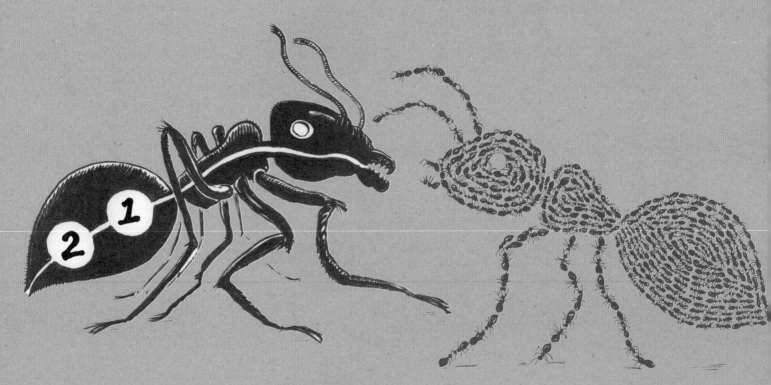

THEY SHARE FOOD WITH THE WHOLE COLONY.

LIFE CYCLE OF THE ANT

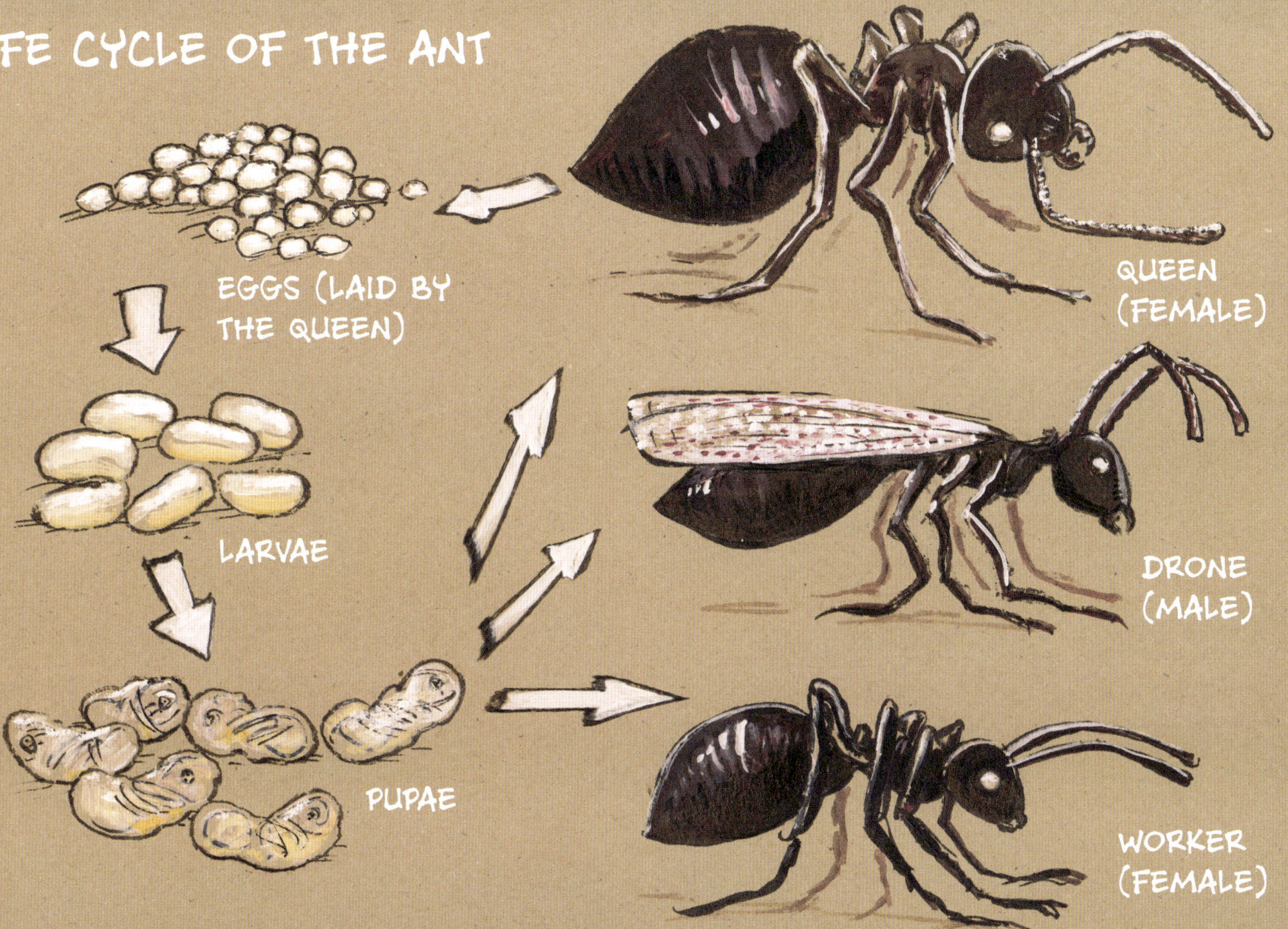
EGGS (LAID BY THE QUEEN)
LARVAE
PUPAE
QUEEN (FEMALE)
DRONE (MALE)
WORKER (FEMALE)

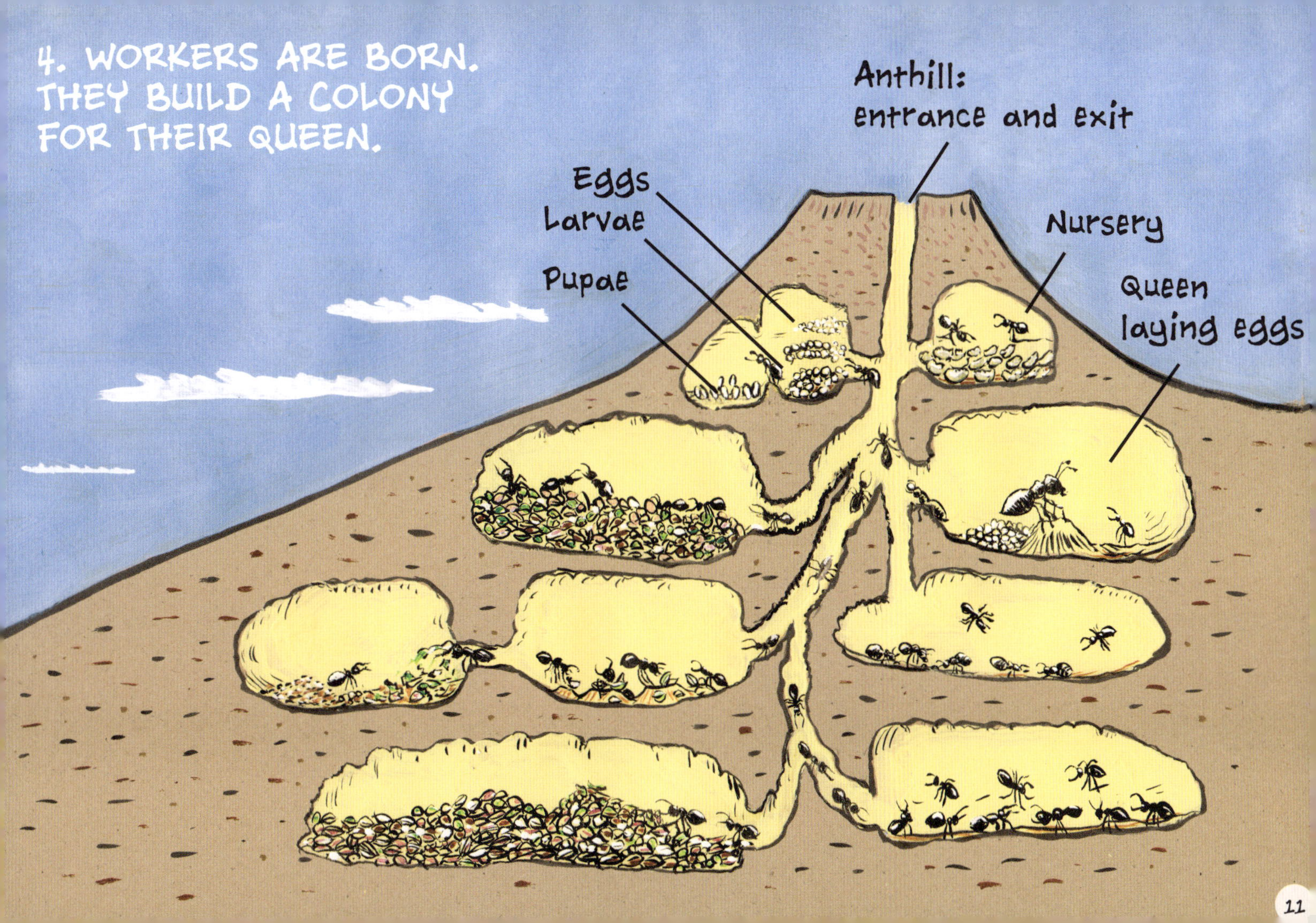
4. WORKERS ARE BORN.
THEY BUILD A COLONY
FOR THEIR QUEEN.
Anthill:
entrance and exit
Eggs
Larvae
Pupae
Nursery
Queen
laying eggs

ANTS DON'T SEE WELL, BUT THEY USE FOUR SENSES:

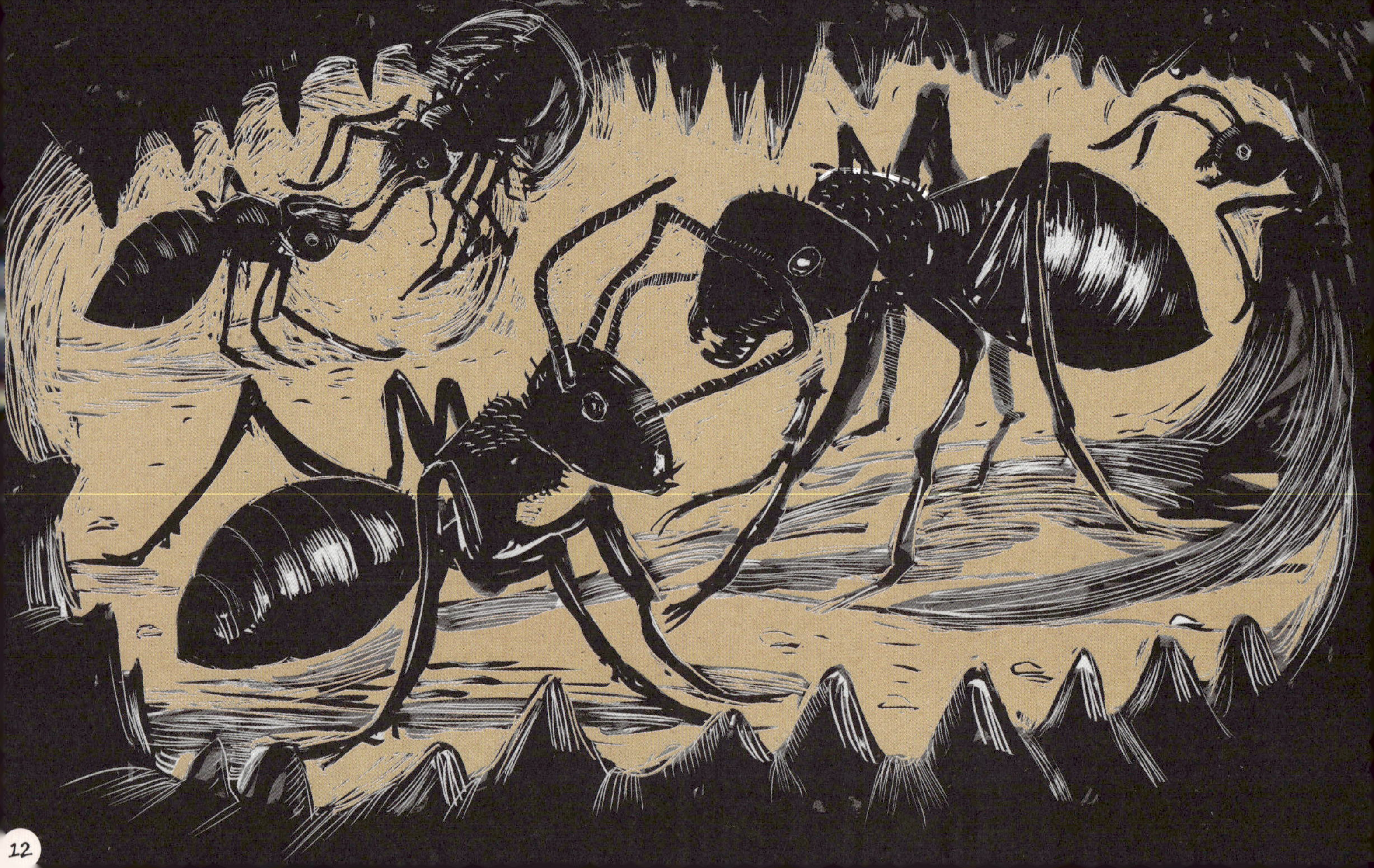

HEARING

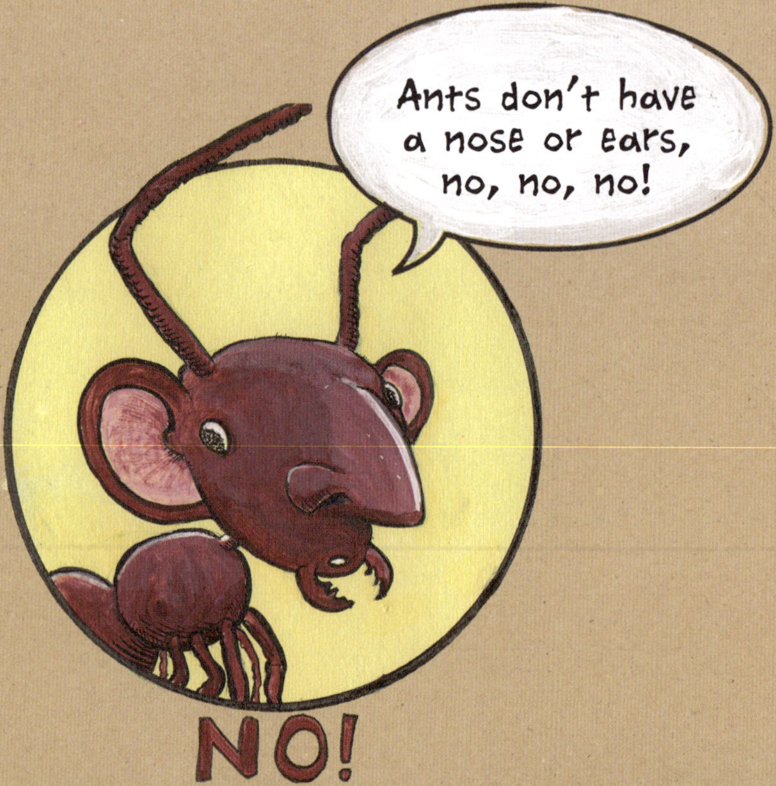

Ants don't have a nose or ears, no, no, no!
NO!

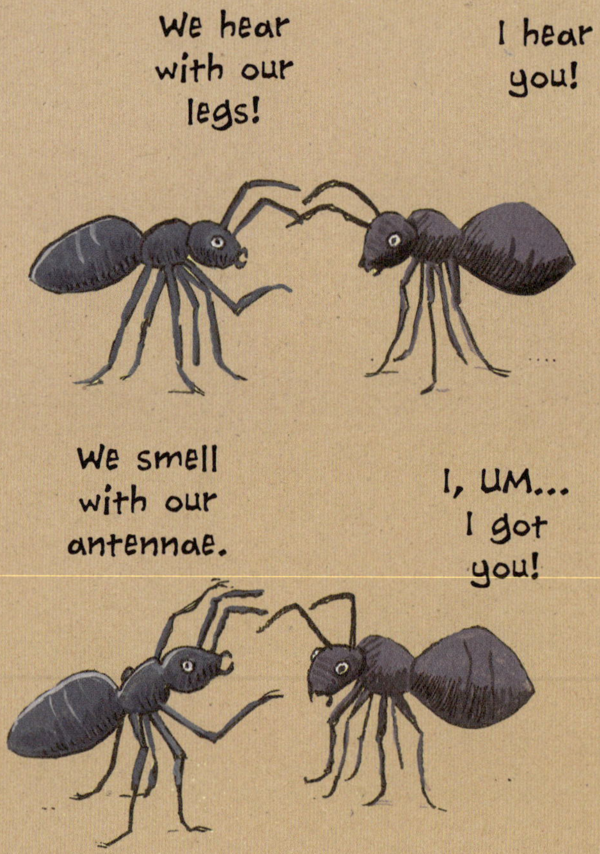

We hear with our legs!
I hear you!
We smell with our antennae.
I, UM... I got you!

Ants feel, hug, and smell with their antennae.

SMELL

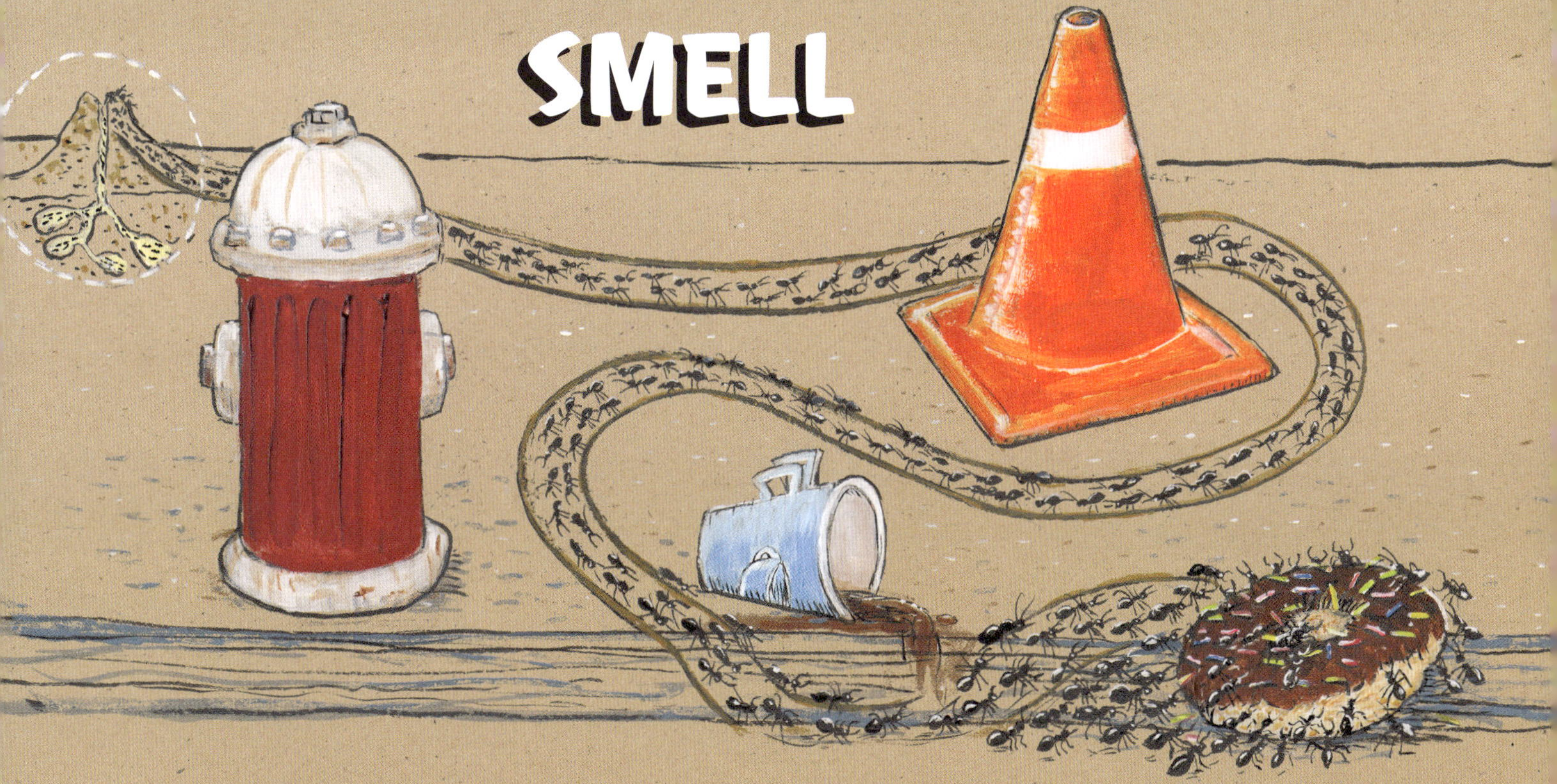

Scout ants bump their bottom to leave a smell trail back to food ( ).

TASTE

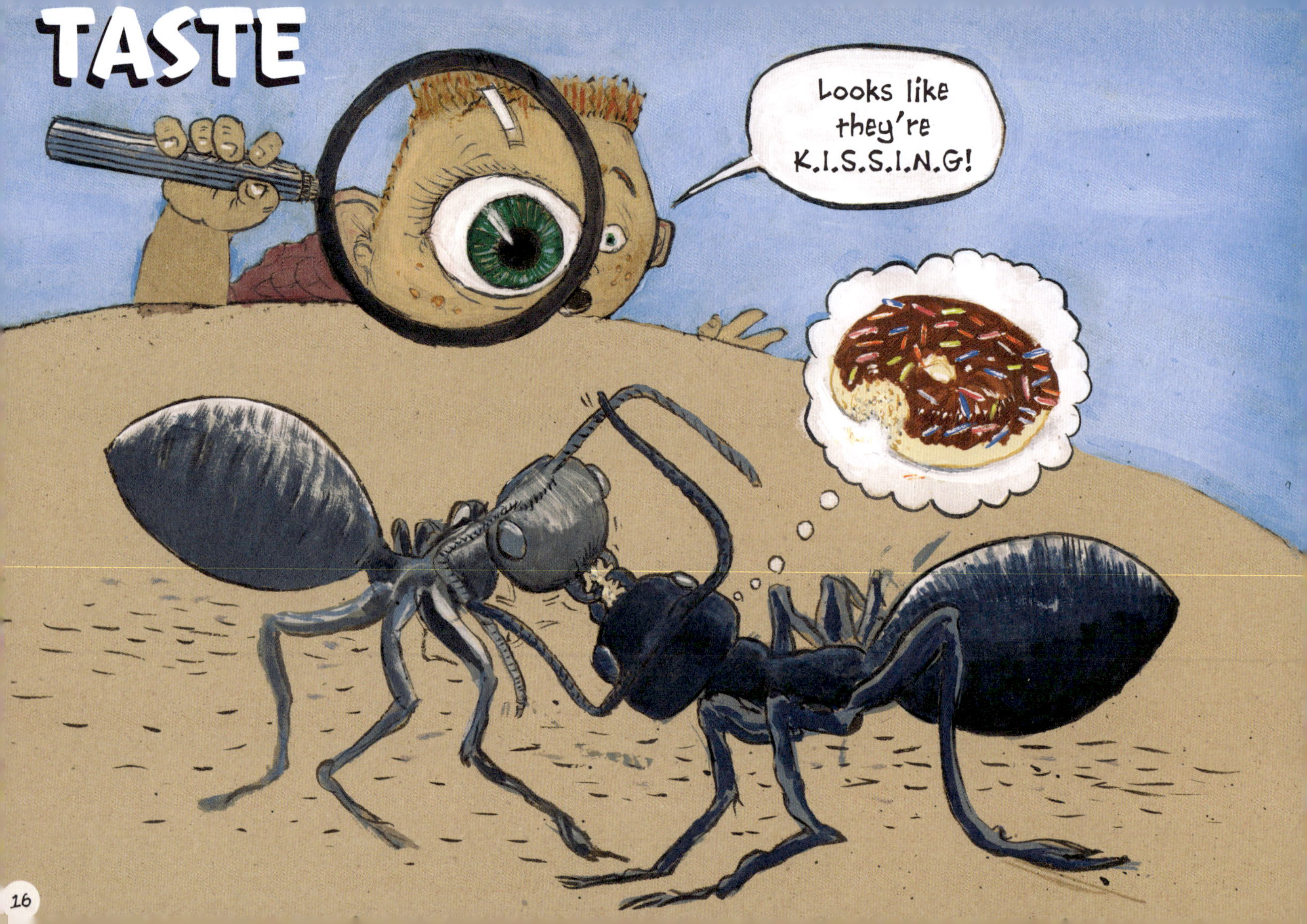
Looks like they're K.I.S.S.I.N.G!

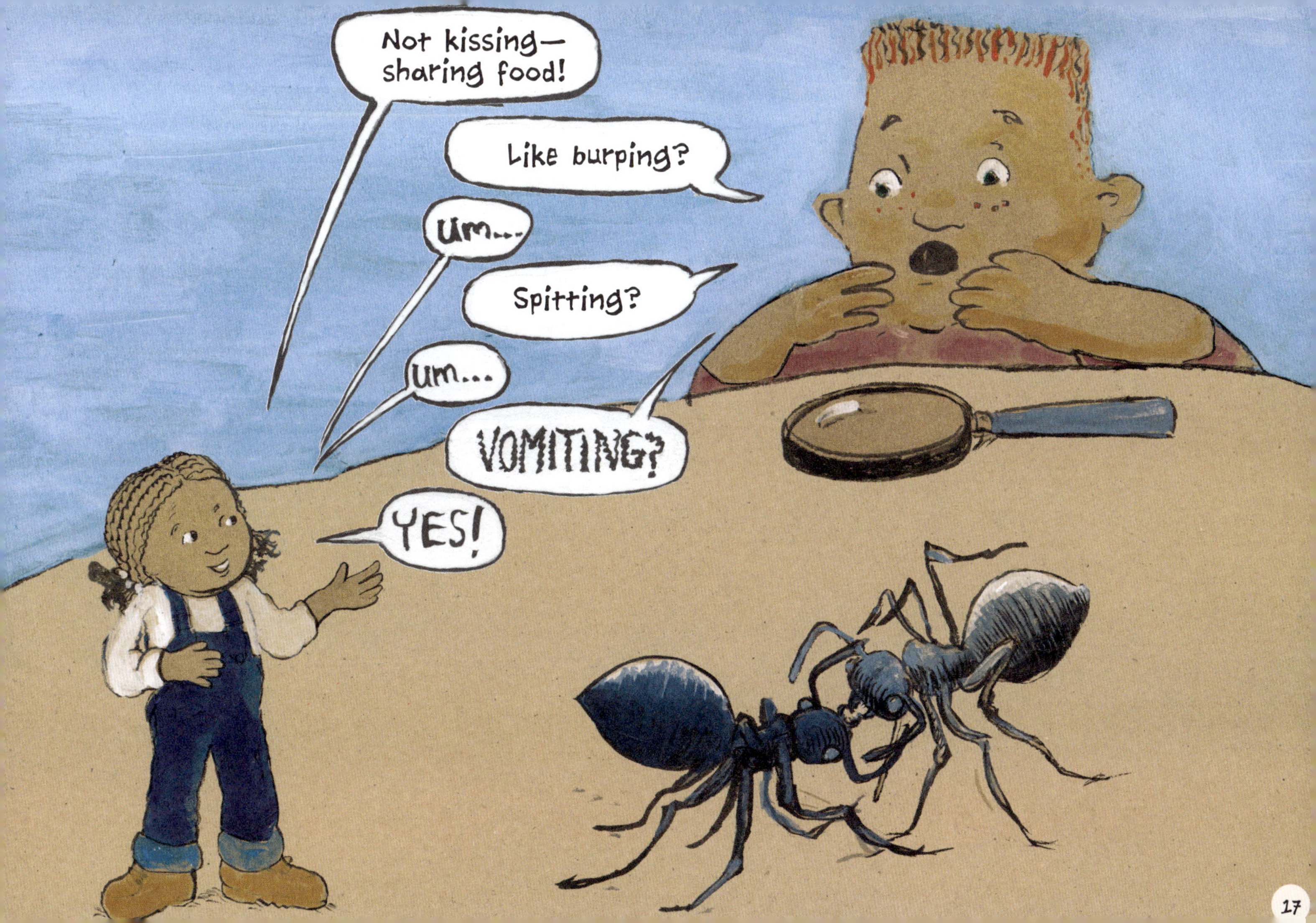
Not kissing—sharing food!
Like burping?
um...
Spitting?
um...
VOMITING?
YES!

AND THERE ARE THOUSANDS OF KINDS OF ANTS:

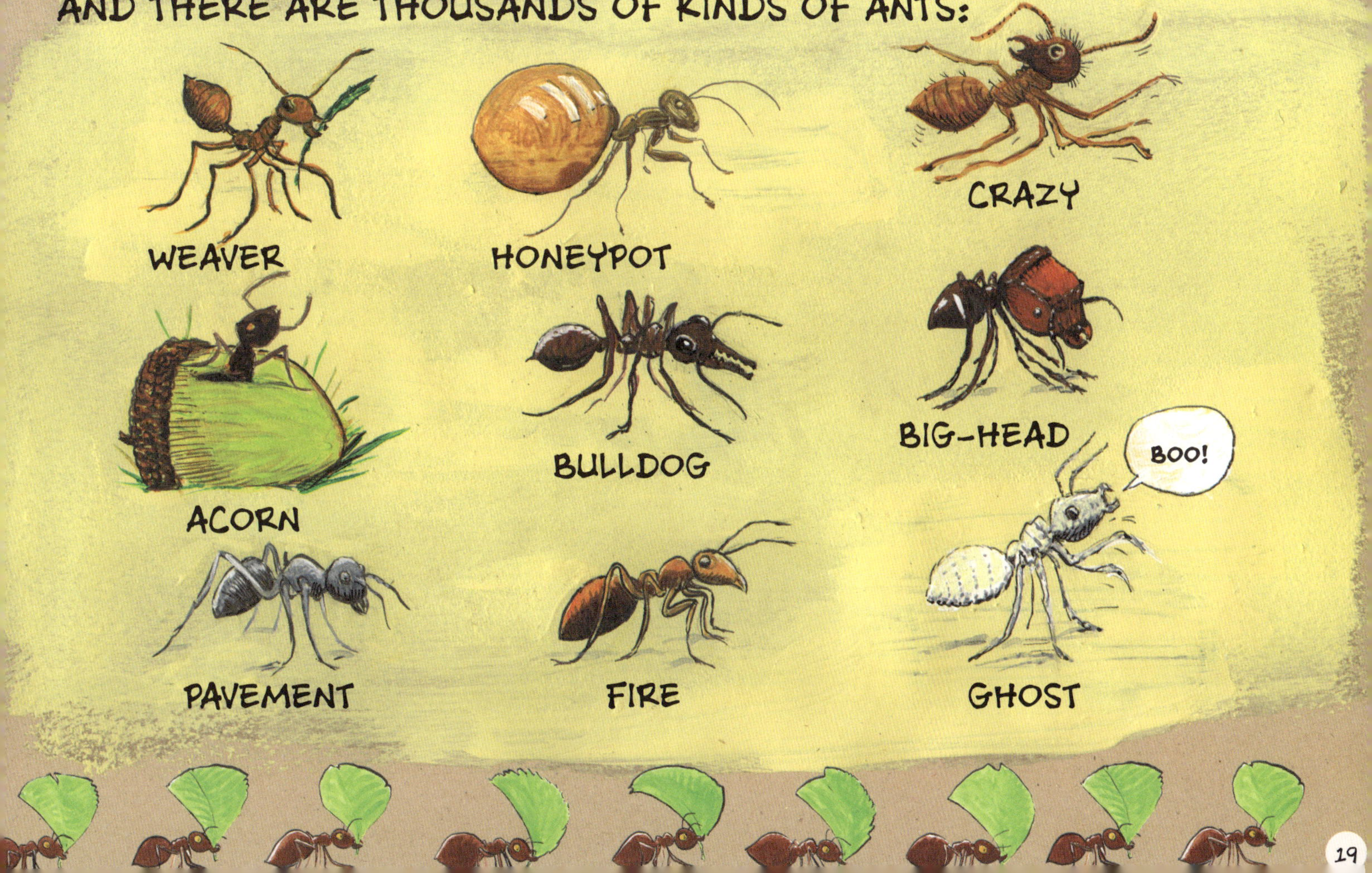
WEAVER
HONEYPOT
CRAZY
ACORN
BULLDOG
BIG-HEAD
BOO!
PAVEMENT
FIRE
GHOST

LEAF-CUTTER ANTS WORK TOGETHER TO FARM.

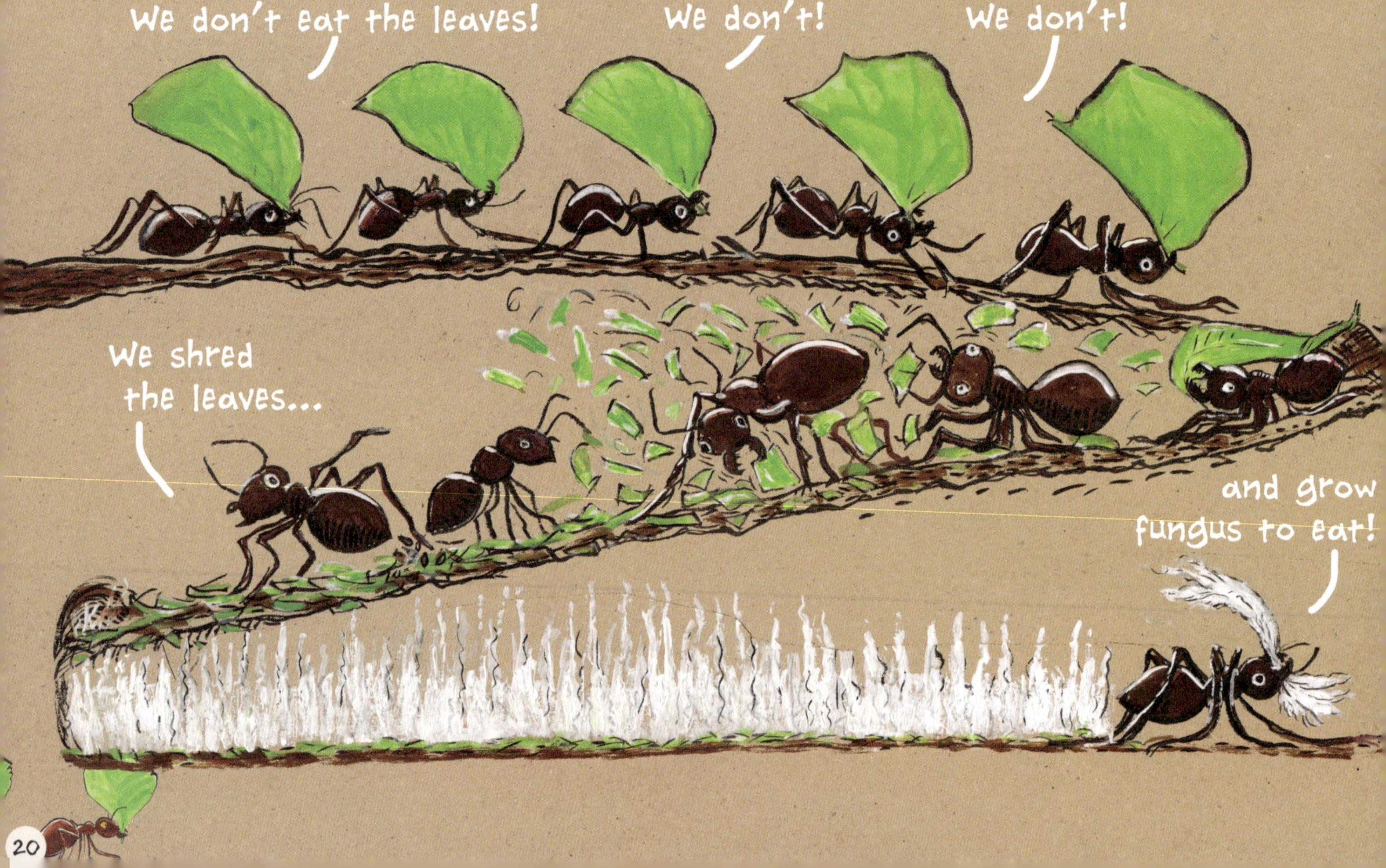
We don't eat the leaves!
We don't!
We don't!
We shred the leaves...
and grow fungus to eat!

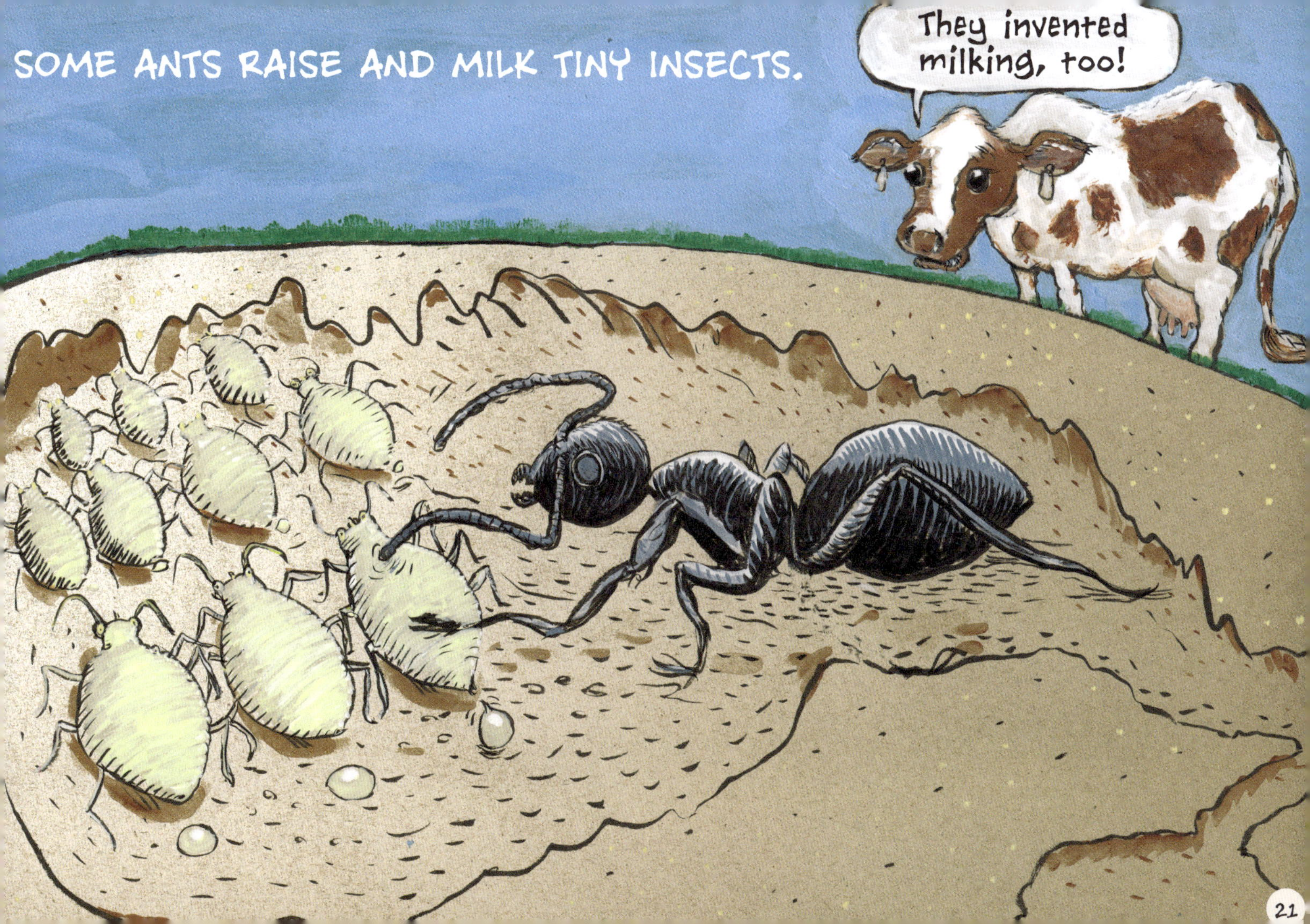
SOME ANTS RAISE AND MILK TINY INSECTS.
They invented milking, too!

A TRAP-JAW ANT CLOSES
ITS JAWS VERY, VERY FAST.

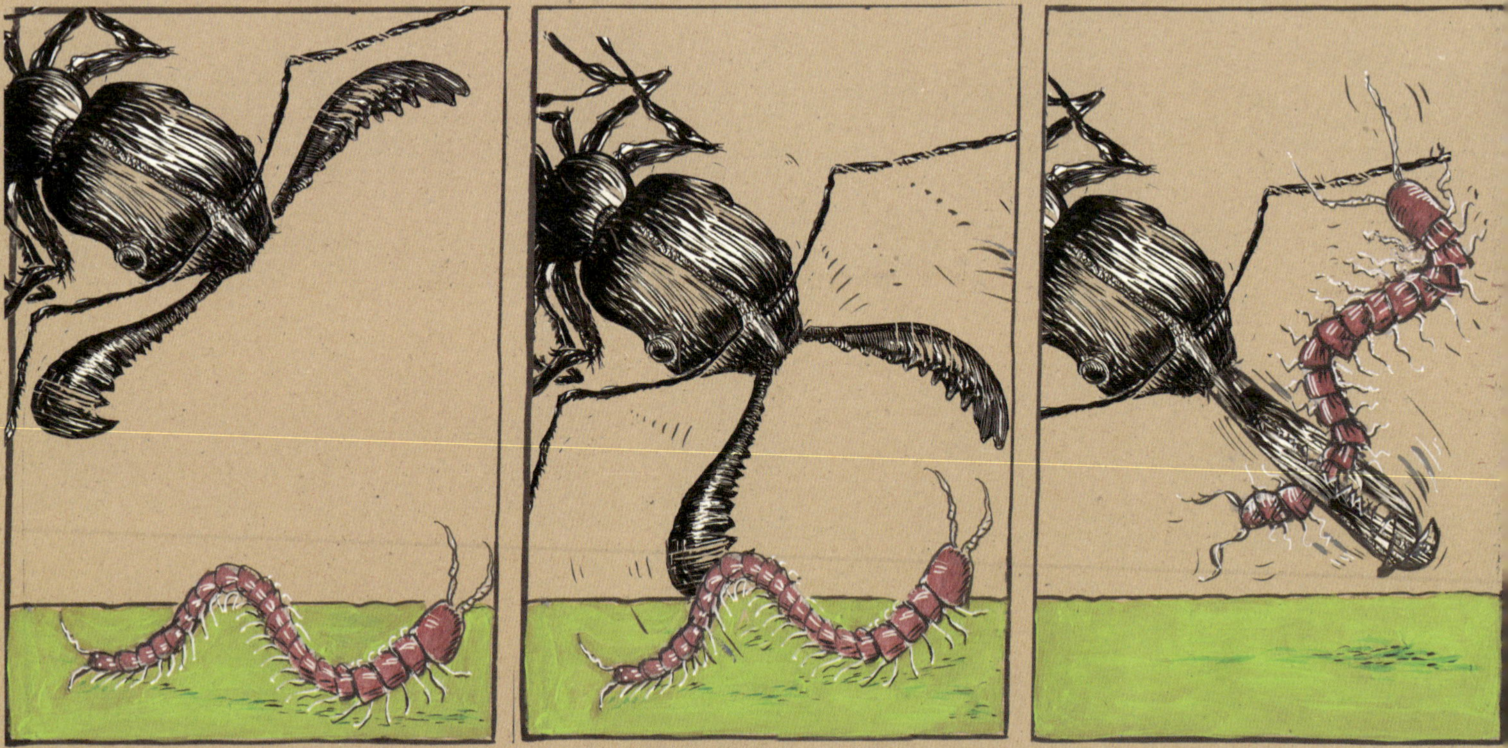

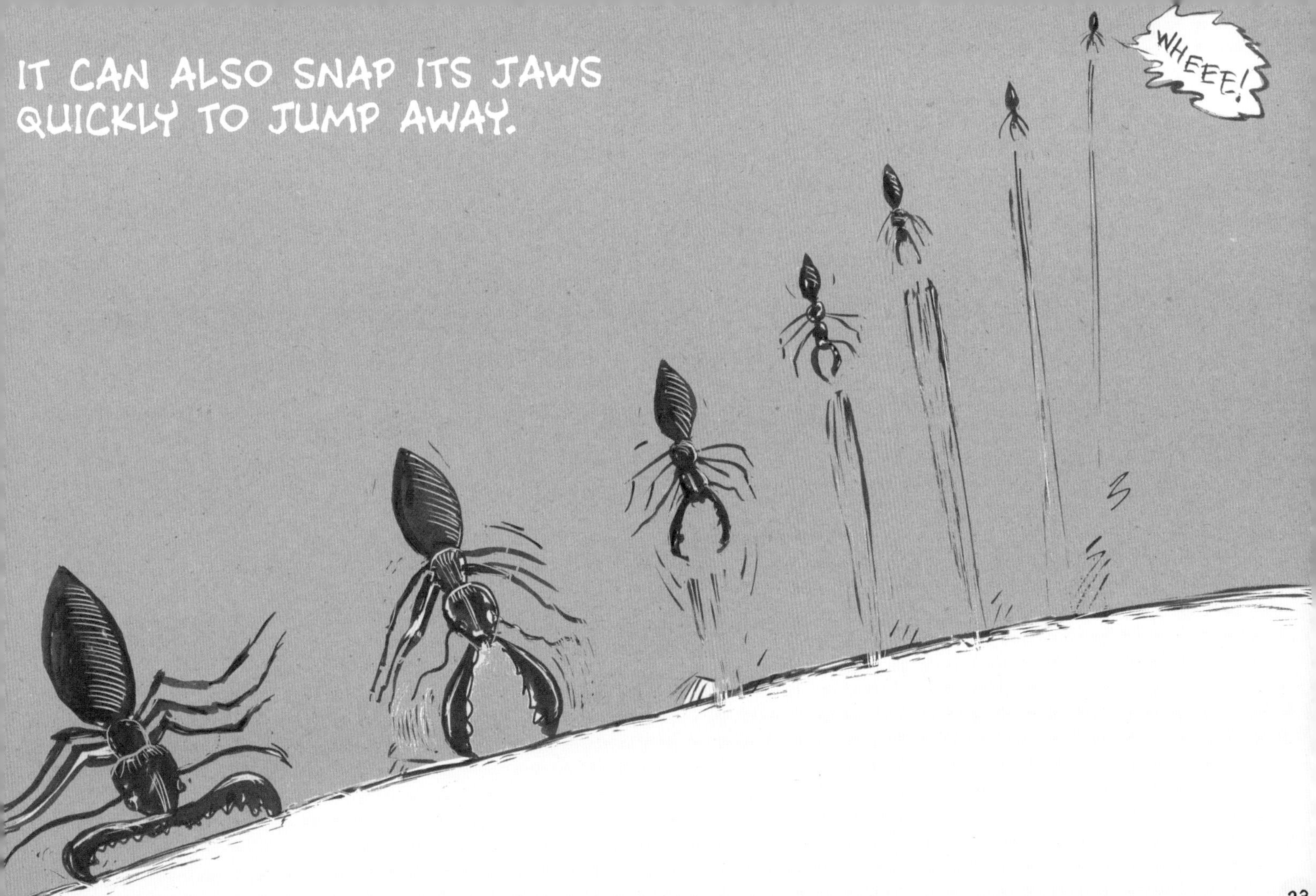
IT CAN ALSO SNAP ITS JAWS QUICKLY TO JUMP AWAY.
WHEEEE!

ANTS CAN LIFT UP TO 50 TIMES THEIR OWN WEIGHT.

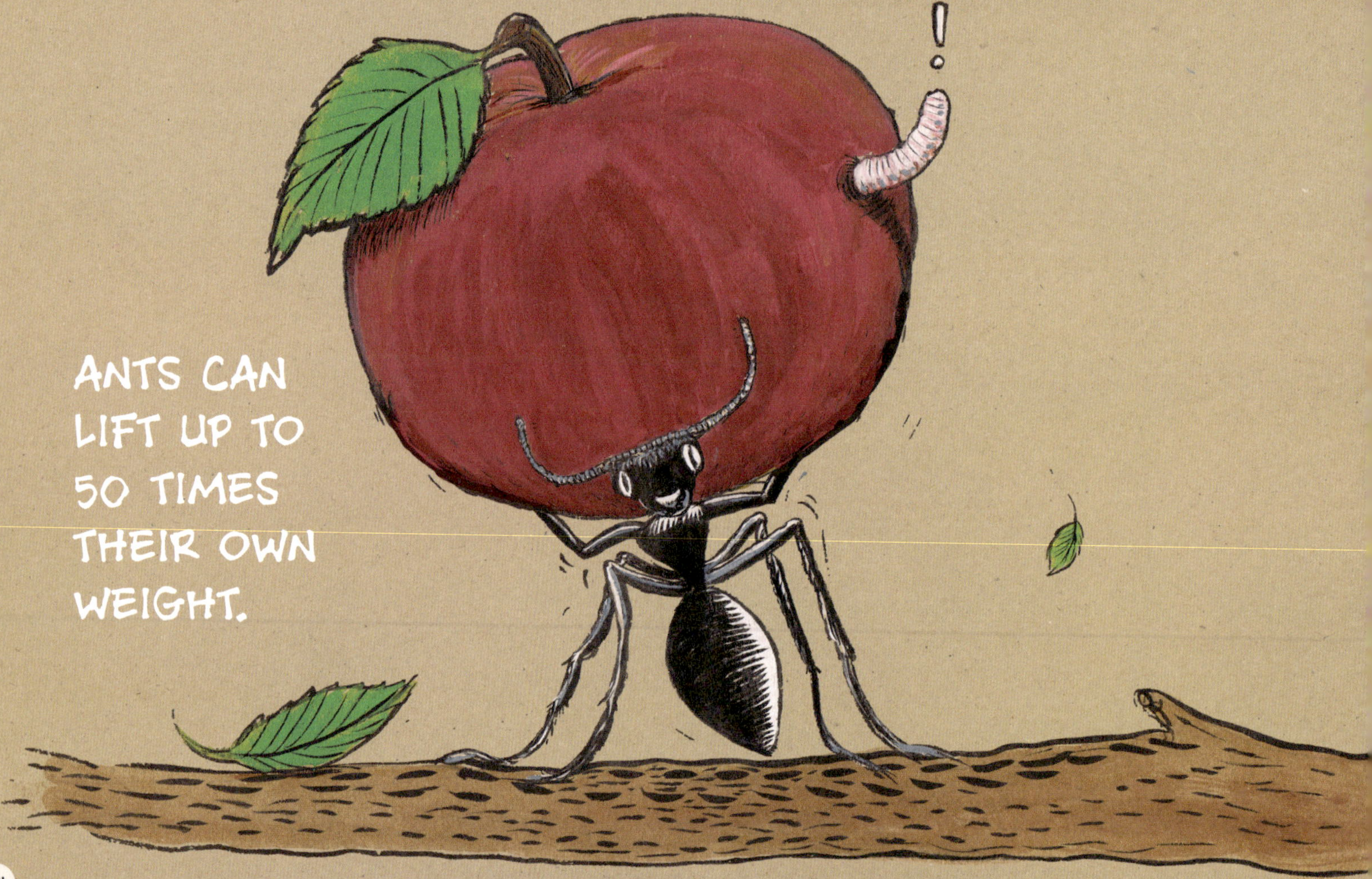

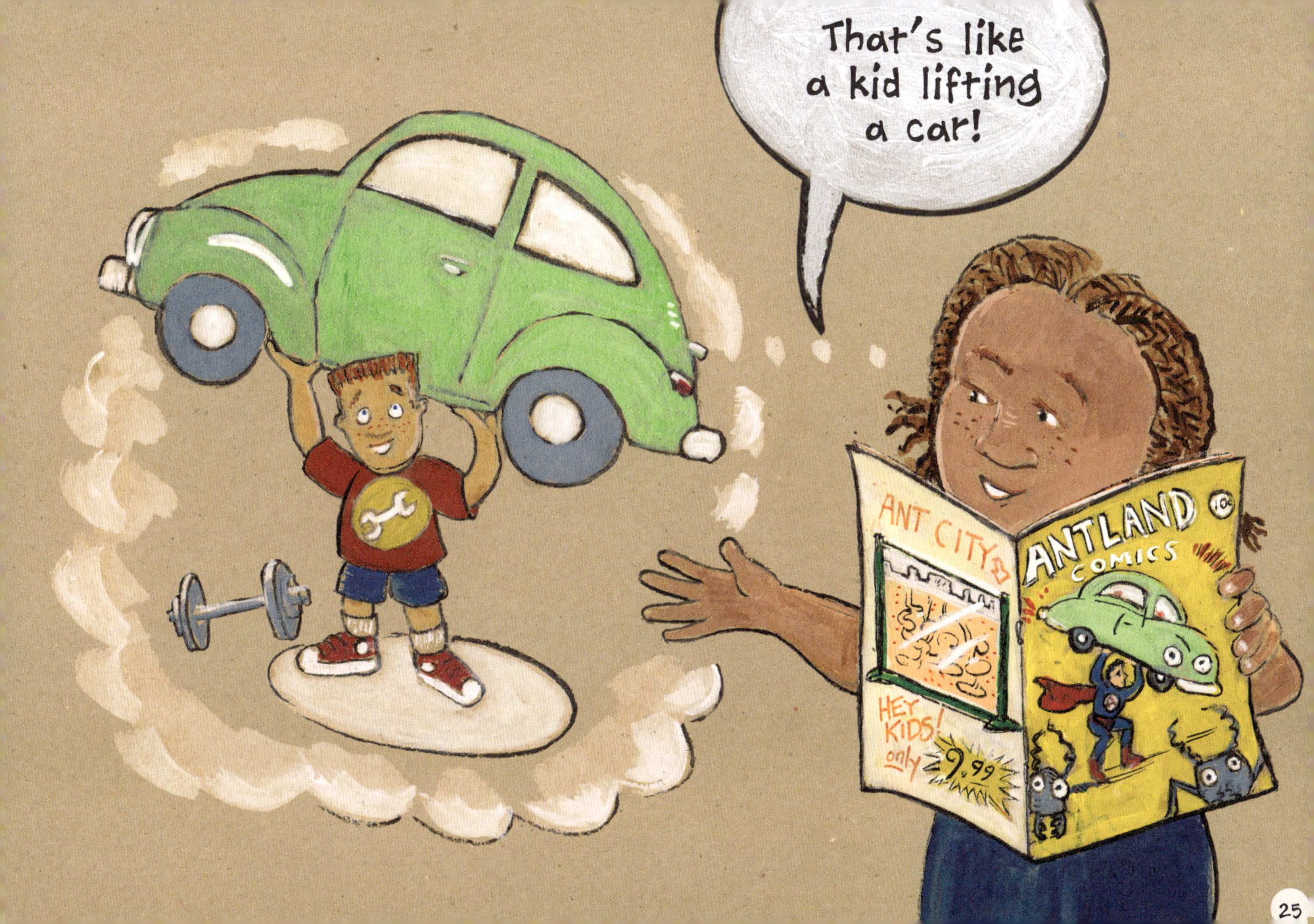
That's like a kid lifting a car!
ANT CITY
ANTLAND
COMICS
10¢
HEY KIDS!
only 9.99

SOME ANTS LIVE IN TREES. ELEPHANTS ARE SCARED OF THEM.

WHAT ANTS EAT...

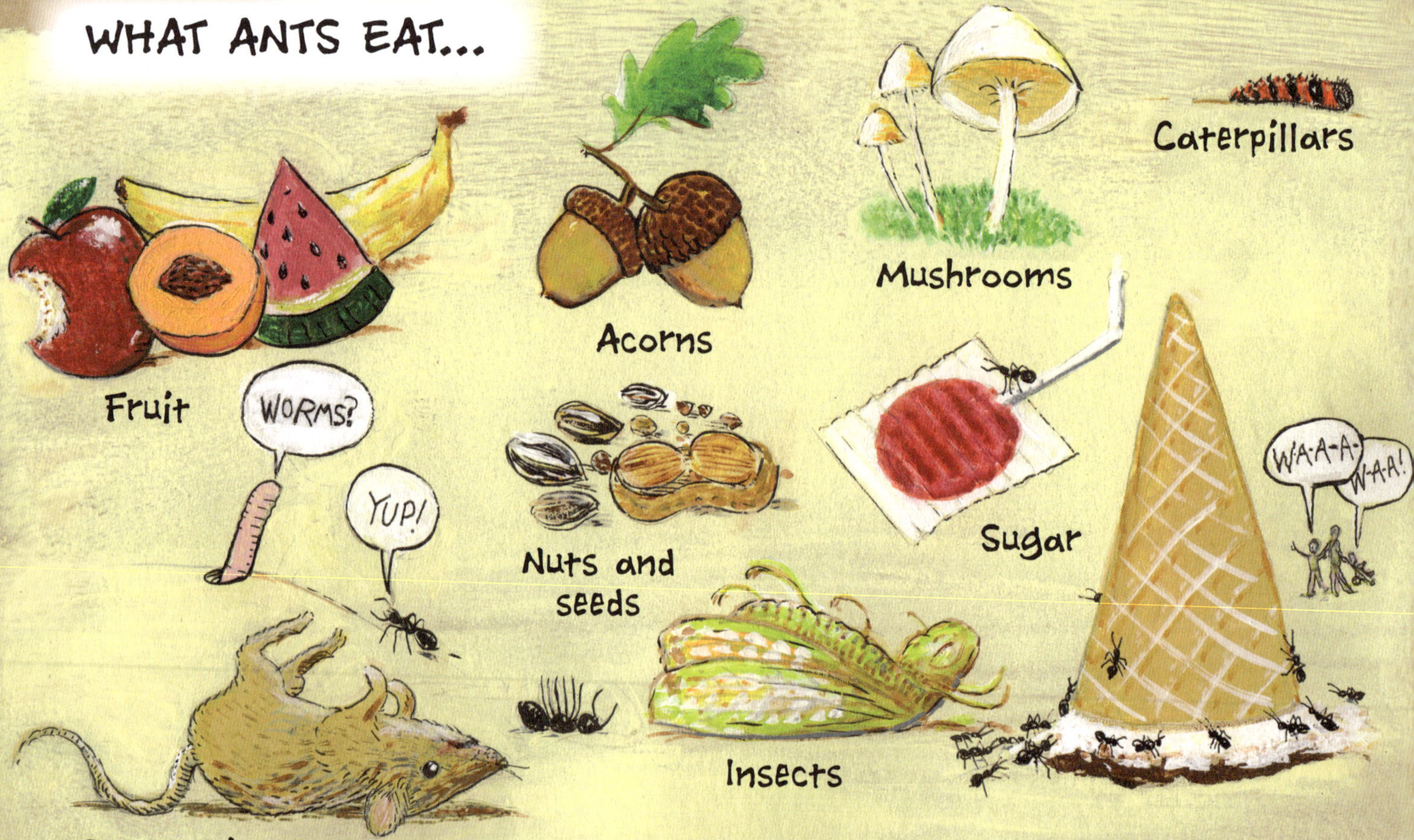
Fruit
Acorns
Mushrooms
Caterpillars
WORMS?
YUP!
Nuts and seeds
Sugar
W-A-A-A-
W-A-A!
Insects
Dead animals

ANTS RECYCLE OUR LEFTOVERS.

WHAT EATS ANTS...

Coyotes

Birds

Snakes

Snails

Venus flytraps

Bears

Salamanders

Frogs

Fish

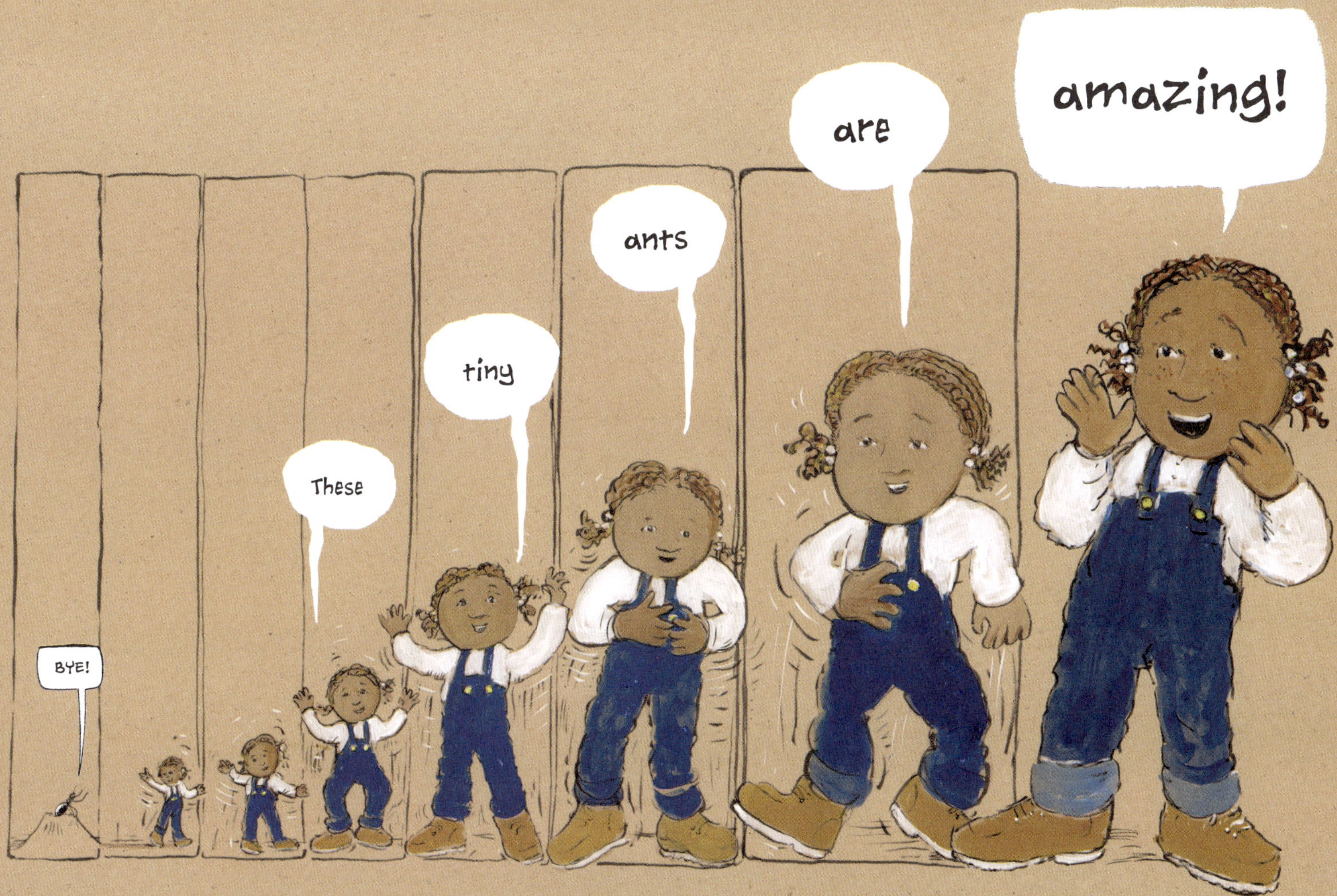
BYE!
These
tiny
ants
are
amazing!